First World War
and Army of Occupation
War Diary
France, Belgium and Germany

30 DIVISION
Divisional Troops
151 Brigade Royal Field Artillery
29 November 1915 - 31 August 1916

WO95/2321/6

The Naval & Military Press Ltd
www.nmarchive.com
Published in association with The National Archives

Published by

The Naval & Military Press Ltd

Unit 10 Ridgewood Industrial Park,

Uckfield, East Sussex,

TN22 5QE England

Tel: +44 (0) 1825 749494

www.naval-military-press.com

www.nmarchive.com

This diary has been reprinted in facsimile from the original. Any imperfections are inevitably reproduced and the quality may fall short of modern type and cartographic standards.

© **Crown Copyright**
Images reproduced by permission of The National Archives, London, England, 2015.

Contents

Document type	Place/Title	Date From	Date To
Heading	WO95/2321/6 151st Bde RFA Nov 1915-Aug 1916		
Heading	30th Division Divl Artillery 151st Bde. R.F.A. Nov 1915-Aug 1916 Broken Up Sept 1916		
Heading	30th Div 157th Bde. R.F.A. Vol. I		
Heading	30 Division		
War Diary	Larkhill Salisbury	29/11/1915	29/11/1915
War Diary	Havre	30/11/1915	01/12/1915
War Diary	Doullens	02/12/1915	02/12/1915
War Diary	St. Ouen	03/12/1915	07/12/1915
War Diary	Puchvillers	08/12/1915	08/12/1915
War Diary	Mailly Maillet	08/12/1915	31/12/1915
Heading	151th Bde R.F.A. Vol 2		
War Diary	St. Ouen	01/01/1916	18/01/1916
War Diary	Suzanne	16/01/1916	18/01/1916
War Diary	Bray	21/01/1916	22/01/1916
War Diary	C/151 Bray	22/01/1916	22/01/1916
War Diary	D/151 Suzanne	22/01/1916	22/01/1916
War Diary	A/151 Bray	23/01/1916	23/01/1916
War Diary	B/151 Suzanne	23/01/1916	23/01/1916
War Diary	C/151 Bray	23/01/1916	23/01/1916
War Diary	D/151 Suzanne	23/01/1916	23/01/1916
War Diary	A/151 Bray	24/01/1916	24/01/1916
War Diary	B/151 Suzanne	24/01/1916	24/01/1916
War Diary	C/151 Bray	24/01/1916	24/01/1916
War Diary	D/151 Suzanne	24/01/1916	24/01/1916
War Diary	A/151 Bray	25/01/1916	25/01/1916
War Diary	B/151 Suzanne	25/01/1916	25/01/1916
War Diary	C/151 Bray	25/01/1916	25/01/1916
War Diary	D/151 Suzanne	25/01/1916	25/01/1916
War Diary	A/151 Bray	26/01/1916	26/01/1916
War Diary	B/157 Suzanne	26/01/1916	26/01/1916
War Diary	C/151 Bray	26/01/1916	27/01/1916
War Diary	D/151	26/01/1916	26/01/1916
War Diary	A/151 Bray	27/01/1916	27/01/1916
War Diary	B/151 Suzanne	27/01/1916	27/01/1916
War Diary	D/151 Suzanne	27/01/1916	27/01/1916
War Diary	A/157 Bray	28/01/1916	28/01/1916
War Diary	B/157 Suzanne	28/01/1916	28/01/1916
War Diary	C/157	28/01/1916	28/01/1916
War Diary	D/157 Suzanne	28/01/1916	28/01/1916
War Diary	A/151 Bray	29/01/1916	29/01/1916
War Diary	B/151 Suzanne	29/01/1916	29/01/1916
War Diary	C/151 Bray	29/01/1916	29/01/1916
War Diary	D/151 Suzanne	29/01/1916	29/01/1916
War Diary	A/151	30/01/1916	30/01/1916
War Diary	B/151	30/01/1916	30/01/1916
War Diary	D/151	30/01/1916	30/01/1916
War Diary	A/151	31/01/1916	31/01/1916
War Diary	C/151	31/01/1916	31/01/1916
War Diary	D/151	31/01/1916	31/01/1916

War Diary	A/151 Bray		01/02/1916	01/02/1916
War Diary	B/151 Suzanne		01/02/1916	01/02/1916
War Diary	C/157 Bray		01/02/1916	01/02/1916
War Diary	D/151		01/02/1916	01/02/1916
War Diary	A/157 Bray		02/02/1916	02/02/1916
War Diary	B/157 Suzanne		02/02/1916	02/02/1916
War Diary	C/151 Bray		02/02/1916	02/02/1916
War Diary	D/151 Suzanne		02/02/1916	02/02/1916
War Diary	A/151 Bray		03/02/1916	03/02/1916
War Diary	B/151		03/02/1916	03/02/1916
War Diary	A/151		03/02/1916	03/02/1916
War Diary	Bray		03/02/1916	04/02/1916
War Diary	D/151 Suzanne		03/02/1916	03/02/1916
War Diary	B/157 Suzanne		04/02/1916	04/02/1916
War Diary	A/151 Bray		04/02/1916	04/02/1916
War Diary	D/151 Suzanne		04/02/1916	06/02/1916
War Diary	A/151		04/02/1916	04/02/1916
War Diary	B/151		04/02/1916	04/02/1916
War Diary	D/151 Suzanne		04/02/1916	05/02/1916
War Diary	A/157		06/02/1916	06/02/1916
War Diary				
War Diary	B/151		06/02/1916	06/02/1916
War Diary	Section B/151 Left Group		06/02/1916	06/02/1916
War Diary	D/151		06/02/1916	06/02/1916
War Diary	Bray		06/02/1916	06/02/1916
War Diary	A/151		07/02/1916	07/02/1916
War Diary	B/151		07/02/1916	07/02/1916
War Diary	D/151		07/02/1916	07/02/1916
War Diary	A/151		08/02/1916	08/02/1916
War Diary	B/151		08/02/1916	08/02/1916
War Diary	D/151		08/02/1916	08/02/1916
War Diary	A/151		09/02/1916	09/02/1916
War Diary	B/151		09/02/1916	09/02/1916
War Diary	D/151		09/02/1916	09/02/1916
War Diary	A/151		10/02/1916	10/02/1916
War Diary	B/151		10/02/1916	10/02/1916
War Diary	D/151		10/02/1916	10/02/1916
War Diary	A/151		11/02/1916	11/02/1916
War Diary	B/151		11/02/1916	11/02/1916
War Diary	D/151		11/02/1916	11/02/1916
War Diary	A B D/151		12/02/1916	12/02/1916
War Diary	A/151		13/02/1916	13/02/1916
War Diary	B/151		13/02/1916	13/02/1916
War Diary	D/151		13/02/1916	13/02/1916
War Diary	A/151		14/02/1916	14/02/1916
War Diary	B/151		14/02/1916	14/02/1916
War Diary	D/151		14/02/1916	14/02/1916
War Diary	A B D/151		15/02/1916	15/02/1916
War Diary	A B T D/151		16/02/1916	18/02/1916
War Diary	A/151		19/02/1916	19/02/1916
War Diary	B/151		19/02/1916	19/02/1916
War Diary	D/151		19/02/1916	19/02/1916
War Diary	A/151		20/02/1916	20/02/1916
War Diary	B/151		20/02/1916	20/02/1916
War Diary	D/151		20/02/1916	20/02/1916
War Diary	A/151		21/02/1916	21/02/1916

War Diary	B/151	21/02/1916	21/02/1916
War Diary	D/151	21/02/1916	21/02/1916
War Diary	A/151	22/02/1916	22/02/1916
War Diary	B/151	22/02/1916	22/02/1916
War Diary	A/151 B/151 D/151	23/02/1916	23/02/1916
War Diary	A B & D/151	24/02/1916	24/02/1916
War Diary	D/151	24/02/1916	24/02/1916
War Diary	Bray A/151	25/02/1916	25/02/1916
War Diary	B/151 & Hdqrs 151	26/02/1916	26/02/1916
War Diary	151/BAC	27/02/1916	28/02/1916
War Diary	A & B/151	29/02/1916	29/02/1916
War Diary	D/151	29/02/1916	29/02/1916
War Diary	A	01/03/1916	01/03/1916
War Diary	B	01/03/1916	01/03/1916
War Diary	D	01/03/1916	01/03/1916
War Diary	A/157	02/03/1916	02/03/1916
War Diary	B/151	02/03/1916	03/03/1916
War Diary	D/151	02/03/1916	02/03/1916
War Diary	A/151	03/03/1916	03/03/1916
War Diary	B/151	03/03/1916	03/03/1916
War Diary	D/151	03/03/1916	03/03/1916
War Diary	A/151 B/151 D/151	04/03/1916	04/03/1916
War Diary	A/151	05/03/1916	05/03/1916
War Diary	B/151	05/03/1916	05/03/1916
War Diary	D/151	05/03/1916	05/03/1916
War Diary	ABD/151	06/03/1916	06/03/1916
War Diary	A/151	07/03/1916	07/03/1916
War Diary	B/151	07/03/1916	07/03/1916
War Diary	D/151	07/03/1916	07/03/1916
War Diary	A/151	08/03/1916	08/03/1916
War Diary	B/151	08/03/1916	08/03/1916
War Diary	D/151	09/03/1916	10/03/1916
War Diary	ABD/151	11/03/1916	11/03/1916
War Diary	A/151	12/03/1916	12/03/1916
War Diary	B/151	12/03/1916	12/03/1916
War Diary	D/151	12/03/1916	12/03/1916
War Diary	A/151	13/03/1916	13/03/1916
War Diary	B/151	13/03/1916	13/03/1916
War Diary	D/151	13/03/1916	13/03/1916
War Diary		14/03/1916	28/03/1916
War Diary	A.B & D/151	26/04/1916	26/04/1916
War Diary	A/151	28/04/1916	28/04/1916
War Diary	A.B & D/151		
War Diary	A.B. & D Batteries 151 at Bde		
War Diary	A/151		
War Diary	D/151		
War Diary	B/151		
War Diary	A	02/05/1916	21/05/1916
War Diary	B	21/05/1916	21/05/1916
War Diary	B/151	21/05/1916	21/05/1916
War Diary	D	11/05/1916	21/05/1916
War Diary	Bois-Des-Tailles	21/05/1916	21/05/1916
War Diary	A/151	21/05/1916	21/05/1916
War Diary	B/151	21/05/1916	31/05/1916
War Diary	C/151	21/05/1916	29/05/1916
War Diary	Bois-des-Tailles R/151	01/06/1916	01/07/1916

War Diary	C/151	01/06/1916	30/06/1916
War Diary	B/151	24/06/1916	24/06/1916
War Diary	A/151 30th Div Arty	01/07/1916	27/07/1916
War Diary	A/151	22/07/1916	27/07/1916
War Diary	B/151	01/07/1916	21/07/1916
War Diary	Peronne Road	06/07/1916	31/07/1916
War Diary	C/151	01/07/1916	31/07/1916
Heading	30th Divisional Artillery 151st Brigade Royal Field Artillery. August 1916		
War Diary		18/08/1916	26/08/1916
War Diary	B/151	13/08/1916	30/08/1916
War Diary	A/151	01/08/1916	11/08/1916
War Diary	Bois Des Tailles	01/08/1916	26/08/1916
War Diary	Trench Maricourt	01/08/1916	03/08/1916
War Diary	Daours	04/08/1916	05/08/1916
War Diary	Longeau	06/08/1916	26/08/1916
War Diary	Mt Bernanshon	31/08/1916	31/08/1916
Heading	150 RFA Vol 4		
Heading	151st Bde R.F.A. Vol. 3		
Heading	WO95/2321/7 Jun 1917-Oct 1918 Trench Mortar Supplies		

WO 95
2321.6
151st Bde RFA
Nov. 1915 – Aug 1916

30TH DIVISION
DIVL ARTILLERY

151ST BDE R.F.A.
Nov ~~DEC~~ 1915 – AUG 1916

BROKEN UP
SEPT 1916.

157th Bde: RFA.
Vol. I

131/7931

Dec 1915
Aug 1916

30/1/5/11

WAR DIARY
or
INTELLIGENCE SUMMARY.
(Erase heading not required.)

Army Form C. 2118.

Hour, Date, Place	Summary of Events and Information	Remarks and references to Appendices
Larkhill 29/4. Salisbury	On the evening of this date, the 101st (County Palatine) Howitzer Brigade, R.F.A. consisting of 4 Batteries and Brigade Ammunition Column, commanded by Lieut-Col. C. Lyon, R.F.A., embarked at Southampton for service overseas.	
5 a.m. 30/4/15 Havre.	Anchored off Havre; disembarked at 3.30 p.m. and proceeded to Rest Camp for the night.	
6.30 pm 1/5/15 Havre.	Headquarters, "A" Battery, entrained at Gare des Marchandises for Doullens. B, C & D Batteries & Brigade Column, following at intervals. 24 hours train journey.	

WAR DIARY
or
INTELLIGENCE SUMMARY.
(Erase heading not required.)

Army Form C. 2118.

Hour, Date, Place	Summary of Events and Information	Remarks and references to Appendices
4.30pm. 2/12/15. Doullens.	Headquarters A.Battery arrived at Doullens & detrained. 8pm. left for St. Ouen, passing thro' Lienvillers, Beauval, to Vauchelles, arriving at St. Ouen, at 2.30 a.m. Billets & horses lines. Rained heavily all the way from Doullens. Distance 15/18 miles.	
St. Ouen 3/12/15. " 4/12/15. " 5/12/15. " 6/12/15.	Horses rested. Billeting arrangements completed. Horse lines etc. checked upon for the several units.	
St. Ouen 7/12/15. 9 a.m.	Headquarters "A" & "B" Batteries proceeded by route march to Puchvillers, passing thro' Fignacourt, Villers Bocage, &c. Billeted for the night. Nailed. Proceeded to Maiery. Nailed. Halgro going on in advance, and reported to the Off. 127 How Bde 71. a.m.	
9 a.m. 8/12/15. Puchvillers.		

WAR DIARY
INTELLIGENCE SUMMARY.
(Erase heading not required.)

Army Form C. 2118.

Hour, Date, Place	Summary of Events and Information	Remarks and references to Appendices
@ Mailly Maillet		
5 pm 8/12/15	"A" & "D" Batteries attached to 86th How. Bty R.F.A. & 128th How Bty R.F.A. respectively for instructional purposes. One officer of "A" line at Forceville. 157 Bde Ammn Column attached to "A" & "D" Bde Ammn Column at Forceville for instructions. Route from Puchvillers to Mailly, via Toutencourt, Harponville, Varennes.	
9 am 9/12/15	"A" & "D" Batteries taking up the alternative positions of 86th Bty & 128th Bty. Weather very wet.	As above.
9 am 10/12/15	"A" & "D" Batteries employed in digging gun pits making gun platforms. Weather very wet.	As above.

Stoney /.

Army Form C. 2118.

WAR DIARY
or
INTELLIGENCE SUMMARY.
(Erase heading not required.)

Instructions regarding War Diaries and Intelligence Summaries are contained in F.S. Regs., Part II and the Staff Manual respectively. Title pages will be prepared in manuscript.

4

Hour, Date, Place	Summary of Events and Information	Remarks and references to Appendices
9. am onwards 11/12/16. Mailly Maillet.	Digging gunpits, making gun platforms.	
" 2 pm	D. Battery. Fired at Enemy trenches towards Calvaire registered zero line	
	A. Battery. registered zero line towards Serre.	
10.30 am 12/12/15 Mailly Maillet.	D. Battery. Fired 11 Rounds HE at German communicating trench at R.7.c.25. Map 1/10,000 registered same.	
10.30 am 13/12/15 Mailly Maillet.	A. Battery fired 15 rounds HE at German Redane trench at K.36.c.2.1. + registered.	
" 2.15pm.	D. Battery fired 3 rounds HE at Enemy communication trench R.7.c.3.8. 3 effective. Ground very soft.	

WAR DIARY
INTELLIGENCE SUMMARY

Army Form C. 2118.

5.

Hour, Date, Place	Summary of Events and Information	Remarks and references to Appendices
2.15 pm 13/12/15 Mailly Maillet	"D" Battery (continued). Fired 14 rounds HE @ earthwork (Map 1/20,000) Q.12.6.8.4. 7 rounds effective. Fired 13 rounds at communication trench Q.12.a.8.4. (Map 1/20,000). ground very soft. all the above targets registered.	
10.30 am 14/12/15 Mailly Maillet	A. Battery. Fired 28 rounds at German front line trench NE of Beaumont Village registered on Q5.C.3.8. Fired 20 rounds at German Reserve trench north of road (junction Beaumont registered for Q.6.d.5.1.)	

Army Form C. 2118.

WAR DIARY
or
INTELLIGENCE SUMMARY.
(Erase heading not required.)

Hour, Date, Place	Summary of Events and Information	Remarks and references to Appendices
15/12/15 16 " 17 " Mailly Maillet	Nothing to report. These three days weather very misty and showery. Batteries did not shoot.	
12/15 6pm 18 12/15 9 am Mailly Maillet	Guns of "A" Bty. Batteries were hauled out of action & limbered up. "A" & "B" Batteries departed for St Ouen. "B" & "C" Batteries arrived took up/on the evening/positions of 86th Battery/& alternating/positions of 86th Battery/ 126th Battery respectively. Digging gun pits — Making gun platforms etc.	
19 – 21. 12/15 MAILLY MAILLET.	Batteries did not fire.	
22 12/15	Fired 70 Rounds HE as under (I) 16 rd at Trench K.30.c.77. (II) " " " — Q6.c.61	

WAR DIARY
or
INTELLIGENCE SUMMARY.
(Erase heading not required.)

Army Form C. 2118.

Hour, Date, Place	Summary of Events and Information	Remarks and references to Appendices
23/15 Mailly Maillet	B. Battery (continued) (III) 8 rds at Communicating Trench near Q.6.c.61. (IV) 18 rounds at Trench K.36.c.21. (V) 12 rounds at Trench Q.5.c.7.10. Fire appeared to be effective. C Battery. Registered German beehive Trench Q.6.c.6.2 to Q.6.a.7.4. D Battery. Registered German front line trenches (B.7.c.6.7.) (B.7.c.6.5.7.) German redoubt. Fire very effective. Also	
9am 24/12/15 Mailly Maillet	E Battery did not fire on this date.	

Army Form C. 2118.

WAR DIARY
or
INTELLIGENCE SUMMARY.
(Erase heading not required.)

Hour, Date, Place	Summary of Events and Information	Remarks and references to Appendices
25/12/15 Mailly Maillet	Batteries did no fire.	
26/12/15 — " —	B. Battery. Fired 30 rounds HE. Registered trenches at Q.5.c.2-8 & Q.6.A.5-6. C. Battery. Registered German front line trench - Fired 21 rounds - Fire effective. Registered salient in German front line trench - 5 rounds HE +	
27/12/15	C. Battery. Fired on salient in German front line trenches - 10 rounds HE + B & C Batteries came out of action returned to billets. Brigade in billets	
28/12/15		
29/12/15		

Army Form C. 2118.

WAR DIARY
or
INTELLIGENCE SUMMARY.
(Erase heading not required.)

Instructions regarding War Diaries and Intelligence Summaries are contained in F.S. Regs., Part II. and the Staff Manual respectively. Title pages will be prepared in manuscript.

Hour, Date, Place	Summary of Events and Information	Remarks and references to Appendices
30/12/15	Brigade in Billets.	
31/12/15	"	

Dyer Lieut Col.
Cmdg 157. Arty.
2nd Jan/16.

151 b Bde. R. 7a.
Vol: 2

WAR DIARY
or
INTELLIGENCE SUMMARY.
(Erase heading not required.)

Army Form C. 2118.

Hour, Date, Place	Summary of Events and Information	Remarks and references to Appendices
17th – 10th ST. OUEN.	Brigade in billets.	A.A.
10th ST. OUEN.	"B" "D" Batteries left St Ouen for the line; Column commanded by Lieut. Col. Hon. F.T. Stanley, R.F.A. "B" Brigade Billeted at Tatinghem on the night of 10th Jan'y. "D" Bat Noyelles 11th Jan'y.	
14th ST. OUEN	"A" Battery left this day for the line. Column commanded by Lt Col. Pohlmand R.F.A. 148th Brigade. R.F.A. Billeted at Talmas on night of 14th January. Pont Noyelles 15th Jan'y. on 16th arrived into position in the line.	
18th ST. OUEN	Took up position in the line. Headquarters Staff & C Battery left this day for the line following the same route as the A.B & D	

Army Form C. 2118.

WAR DIARY
or
INTELLIGENCE SUMMARY.
(Erase heading not required.)

Hour, Date, Place	Summary of Events and Information	Remarks and references to Appendices
	Batteries.	
	The Batteries of 151 Brigade were allotted as follows for fighting purposes:-	
	1. B'D. Batteries to the Right group commanded by Lieut- Col. The Hon. Stanley RFA. commanding 149[*] Brigade RFA. This group being at the extreme right of the British Line, adjoining the French.	* Headquarters Suzanne.
	'A' Battery commanded by Capt Currie group[*] RFA.	* Headquarters BRAY.
	Centre group, Lieut Col. G. Mheron RFA. commanding 148th Brigade RFA.	
	'C' Battery, to the Left group[*], commanded by Lieut Col. F Abington RFA. commanding 149th Brigade RFA.	* Headquarters BRAY.
	Signallers of Headquarters staff worked the telephone exchange at	

WAR DIARY
or
INTELLIGENCE SUMMARY.

(Erase heading not required.)

Army Form C. 2118.

Hour, Date, Place	Summary of Events and Information	Remarks and references to Appendices
15/6. Suzanne	BRONFAY FARM. Headquarters billeted at BRAY, also B/ac/151. Headquarters R.A. (30th DIVISION) ETINEHEM. Divisional Artillery commanded by Brig-Genl J.H.S. Y/Bkn. R.A. B/151. Enemy opened fire near Battery position at 4.15pm at intervals of half an hour, until 4.15pm, firing in all about 100 rounds. 2 men killed, eighty wounded. B/151. Reconstruction work.	
17/6 18-20/6.	Attended registering. Quiet. Batteries registering trenches reconstructing dugouts.	
21/6. BRAY	C/151. Registered French Junction $\pm$ 12 A 2.6. 9 rounds HE× also F.N. a 4.6. 5 Rounds HE×	

WAR DIARY
or
INTELLIGENCE SUMMARY.
(Erase heading not required.)

Army Form C. 2118.

Hour, Date, Place	Summary of Events and Information	Remarks and references to Appendices
22/6 BRAY 12.15pm 3. pm	A/151. Fired 8 rounds HE registering Point A.3.a.5.7. Fired 11 rounds HE onto point A.3.c.0.1.3. A.2.b.5.2. in retaliation. Enemy shelled BRONFAY FARM.	
23/6 B/15/BRAY. 10.30 AM. 3.30 pm 6.35 pm	C/151. A.11.30.pm. Fired 8 rounds at Trench junction F.12.A.0.4. Enemy fired 6.5.9 about Wellington Redoubt. Enemy fired about 24 rounds at BRONFAY FARM. Fired 4 rounds at request of infantry at Trench Mortar off about F.10/D.8.6.	
22/6 D/151 SUZANNE-BRAY	Registering.	

Army Form C. 2118.

WAR DIARY
or
INTELLIGENCE SUMMARY.
(Erase heading not required.)

Instructions regarding War Diaries and Intelligence Summaries are contained in F.S. Regs., Part II. and the Staff Manual respectively. Title pages will be prepared in manuscript.

Hour, Date, Place	Summary of Events and Information	Remarks and references to Appendices
23/7/6. BRAY A/151. 4.15 am 12.12 pm.	Fired 11 rounds P.X. at enemy trench A.8.A. a request of infantry. Enemy 77 mm. battery bombarded in aircraft of battery / German balloon up.	
23/7/6. SUZANNE. B/151	A quiet day.	
23/7/6. BRAY. C/151	Nothing to report.	
23/7/6. SUZANNE. D/151.	Enemy balloon up over Bois MEREAUCOURT. Fired 12 rounds at enemy trench, 19 effective.	
24/7/6. BRAY. A 151	Registering. Nothing to report. all quiet.	
24/7/6. SUZANNE. B/151	A quiet day. Nothing to report	

WAR DIARY
or
INTELLIGENCE SUMMARY.
(Erase heading not required.)

Army Form C. 2118.

Instructions regarding War Diaries and Intelligence Summaries are contained in F.S. Regs., Part II. and the Staff Manual respectively. Title pages will be prepared in manuscript.

Hour, Date, Place	Summary of Events and Information	Remarks and references to Appendices
24/9/16 BRAY. C/157.	All quiet.	
24/9/16 SOZANNE. D/161	Fired 50 rounds HE to enemy new structure in trench junction A/23.d.8.3.6.	
25/9/16 BRAY. A/157. 2pm	Fired 50 rounds HE on trenches at I.B.0%. to A.1.B.53. Fired 2 rounds BX at y.3.0 per in B.1. Sector as a test run the Infantry.	
1.10pm	Enemy fired 2 How. Battery fired 6 rounds on communication trench in F.13.c.6.	
4.35 pm	Enemy 77 mm battery fired 6 rounds on Cafney Avenue. Enemy balloons up during the day.	

Army Form C. 2118.

WAR DIARY
or
INTELLIGENCE SUMMARY.
(Erase heading not required.)

Instructions regarding War Diaries and Intelligence Summaries are contained in F. S. Regs., Part II. and the Staff Manual respectively. Title pages will be prepared in manuscript.

Hour, Date, Place	Summary of Events and Information	Remarks and references to Appendices
25/6 B/157 SUZANNE.	Enemy aircraft active over the vicinity of this battery. A 'sausage' towing of MN and another to SE.	
25/6 C/157 BRAY.	Nothing to report.	
25/6 D/157 SUZANNE.	Observation impossible owing to Enemy balloon over Bois de Mylegn which is often seen after Fog had lifted. Enemy aeroplanes flying over position between 2.30 pm & 8.30 pm.	
26/6 A/157 BRAY.	At 11.15 pm fired 6 rounds at rest of Infantry on trenches between A 8 T.A. 34 & T.A 84, otherwise a quiet night. Registered targets.	
26/6 B/157 SUZANNE		
26/6 C/157 BRAY.	Fired 15 Rounds BX on Trench junction at Fn 8 13.9. registered.	

Hour, Date, Place	Summary of Events and Information	Remarks and references to Appendices
26/7/16 D/151. 7.30 am	Registered trench H16 & 2. Sent for Telephonist B.O/C. Right Coy. Scots Fusiliers asking him if agreeable to evacuate Sap 73, Telephonist before 2 sheets of paper on certain ousting at 10.30 am. Fire to begin 10 minutes later. Above plan worked smoothly. Fired 10 rounds HE, observation very good. Machine gun reported destroyed by first round. Sent officer in afternoon to investigate. Emplacement completely destroyed.	
2.30 pm.	Enemy fired 4 rounds twice HE at battery, but without effect.	
1.45 pm - 2.5 pm.	Enemy fired 60 in all about 120 rounds * at battery — all heavy. 562 rounds (579) from direction of MAUREPAS 55 " 18 " (4.2) from direction of HEM de NEM	* Only one man hit.

WAR DIARY
or
INTELLIGENCE SUMMARY.

Army Form C. 2118.

Hour, Date, Place	Summary of Events and Information	Remarks and references to Appendices
27/6 A/151 B/RA 6.55pm 10 am	Registration. A request by Infantry/ fired 4 rounds H.X. on A 8.a/9. 5"/	
B/151 SUZANNE	Registered Target A.3.D.8.7. r A.3.D.9.9. Eg. 30 am. Fired 20 rounds H.X. at aeroplane with instructions 1.25 pm. Target inaccordance with instructions recd.	
D/151 SUZANNE	Very quiet day. 10.30 p.m. — 10.35 p.m. number of cyclists observed on road B.25.A.8.1., moving in direction of CLERY.	
28/6 A/151 FRAY	5.20 am. Fired 20 rounds H.X. on communication trench in retaliation, A.8.a. 6.50 a.m. Fired 30 rounds B.X. on communication trenches in A.4.c + A.3.d. at request of Infantry. 7.am. 40 rounds H.X. of shrapnel fired in A.8.a, at request of Infantry. Line trench in A.8.a, at request of Infantry.	

WAR DIARY
or
INTELLIGENCE SUMMARY.
(Erase heading not required.)

Army Form C. 2118.

Hour, Date, Place	Summary of Events and Information	Remarks and references to Appendices
28/6 A/157 (Continued)	Germans bombarded B1 Sector also French 51 & 52. 5.20 am. Enemy 77 mm. battery shelled BEON FAY FARM. German batteries active all day. Firing on our front line & communication trenches in section Pts. B2 & 93. Flash of a hostile battery observed from Aga. O.S. true bearing 3571 appears to be on edge of MONTEBAN.	
28/6 B/157 SUZANNE	From 13 hrs daylight 27/6 – 28/6 the enemy shelled the vicinity of the battery intermittently to 1/5 pm 28/6. No damage done except to telephone wires. In accordance with orders received from Right Group Commander fired 21 rounds FX into HARDICOURT & during the day Garrison another 50 rounds were fired.	* Signal Gibson RFA. of "B" Battery killed in the trenches at SUZANNE. Buried in SUZANNE CEMETERY the following night HARDICOURT in British portion.

Army Form C. 2118.

WAR DIARY
or
INTELLIGENCE SUMMARY.
(Erase heading not required.)

Instructions regarding War Diaries and Intelligence Summaries are contained in F.S. Regs., Part II and the Staff Manual respectively. Title pages will be prepared in manuscript.

Hour, Date, Place	Summary of Events and Information	Remarks and references to Appendices

2876

9/5/17.

5.30 a.m. Fired 8 rounds BX at F.10.d.4.5 at request of Infantry.

At 6 a.m. two Gunnah Field Batteries opened fire on PRONFAY FARM and WATERLOO JUNCTION. Fire firing at 7 a.m. ceased to have fired up to that time 1/250 rounds each.

10 a.m. Fired 120 rounds BX at Frirch Junction F.12.a.2.5 & F.11.B.85.65 & the support trench in between those two points in retaliation for shelling of trenches 62 to 65.

4.30 p.m. Fired 20 rounds at F.11.a.3.4 at request of Lt/Group.

Heavy Shelling by one natures of German Batteries in sector 6 trenches all morning.

WAR DIARY
or
INTELLIGENCE SUMMARY.
(Erase heading not required.)

Army Form C. 2118.

Hour, Date, Place	Summary of Events and Information	Remarks and references to Appendices
28/6 D/157. SUZANNE	7.40 am. Battery shelled by enemy 5.9 battery. At 8.30 am. lachrymatory shells were fired & continued all morning. By 8.45 am all wires were cut. Shelling very intense. Wires relaid to O.P. but broken again & again. Fired 40 rounds at chateau & trench A 23 c 9.3.5.1 using Reg. direction. 9.30 am 3 Telephonists went out to repair Brigade wire. The men worked till 12.20 repairing wire which was constantly broken. 4.45 pm. Very misty - all quiet. 2.30 am Fired 16 rounds BX on front line enemy trenches. 4.30 am Fired 16 rounds to support hostile attack along our opposite 51 Infantry.	
29/6 A/157 BRAY		

WAR DIARY
or
INTELLIGENCE SUMMARY.

(Erase heading not required.)

Army Form C. 2118.

Hour, Date, Place	Summary of Events and Information	Remarks and references to Appendices
29/6 A/151 (Continued)	6.15am. Bombing attack on B's Sector (Trenches 50 & 51).	
	6.10 am. Received warning of Gas attack. Gas only just perceptible, due to few of shells apparently fired at SUZANNE.	
	2.40pm. Fired 24 rounds AX slow rate in retaliation for German shelling.	
29/6 B/151 SUZANNE	Enemy shelled near the Battery position at intervals during the day/but no damage done.	
29/6 C/151 BRAY	Nothing to report. Quiet night.	
29/6 D/151 SUZANNE	Nothing to report.	

WAR DIARY
or
INTELLIGENCE SUMMARY.
(Erase heading not required.)

Army Form C. 2118.

Hour, Date, Place	Summary of Events and Information	Remarks and references to Appendices
30/10 A/157	Nothing to report. Foggy.	B/157 began line shoot of SUZANNE WOOD between 11 + 12 pm this day. Two of our own wounded. A French line was blown up at 13015. DES TAILLES
" B/157	After which 3 range fired near Battery.	
" C/157.	Nothing to report. Very quiet.	
" D/157	8" siege reported a fire started in trenches, which severe. Fired 8 more rounds — efforts to extinguish fire ceased. Fire burned till 9.20 hrs.	
31/10 A/157	Quiet night. Misty all day.	
" B/157.	Registered target in VA 23.c.7.9.+8.9.+ in accordance with instructions received from Right Group commander. Fired 20 rounds into HARDICOURT — result of this was satisfactory. 3 or 4 houses badly hit.	

Army Form C. 2118.

WAR DIARY
or
INTELLIGENCE SUMMARY.

(Erase heading not required.)

Instructions regarding War Diaries and Intelligence Summaries are contained in F.S. Regs., Part II. and the Staff Manual respectively. Title pages will be prepared in manuscript.

Hour, Date, Place	Summary of Events and Information	Remarks and references to Appendices
2/7/16 C/157	A quiet day. Registered on Fa 11.a.0.35.	
D/157.	Quiet entirely.	

In the field
3.7.16.

Anson Lieut Col
RMA
Cmdg 157. Arty

Army Form C. 2118.

WAR DIARY
or
INTELLIGENCE SUMMARY.
(Erase heading not required.)

Hour, Date, Place	Summary of Events and Information	Remarks and references to Appendices
1/2/16 A/157 B.BAY.	12.45pm (3176-178). Fired 15 rounds PX on F12a. 23. obtained two direct hits. Quantity of timber blown out of trench. Fired 23 rounds PX into MAMETZ and 17 rounds PX in to Tranchée at A8a 7.5. installation 7.15pm. Very misty all day, observation beyond our own trenches difficult.	Lieut. T. Greenwood 14th West Lancs R.F.A. attached to A/157 for a course of Instruction in rifle. 14th Feby 1916.
1/2/16 B/157 SUZANNE	A quiet day, spent in re-construction work. Registered a target on trench A11 a 35.7.	
1/2/16 C/157 B.BAY	Fired 20 rounds PX at F11 a 22.43. FR a. 13. 53. & 30 rounds at MAMETZ in retaliation for shelling of CARNOY.	
1/2/16 D/157.	Misty and quiet.	

WAR DIARY
or
INTELLIGENCE SUMMARY.
(Erase heading not required.)

Army Form C. 2118.

Hour, Date, Place	Summary of Events and Information	Remarks and references to Appendices
2/7 17/157 BRAY	A quiet night. 10.30 a.m. Fired 25 rounds on trenches in subsection B.1. & B.2 registered targets. At 5.30 pm Enemy fired a number of rounds in the direction of BILLON WOOD.	
2/7 B/157 SUZANNE	Quiet. Day spent in reconnaissance work.	
2/7 C/157 BRAY.	At 3pm. Fired 15 rounds attracting gun emplacement F.17.5.2.2. at request of Infantry.	
2/7 D/157 SUZANNE×	Quiet day. Fired 7 rounds at working party A.24.d.2.32.	
3/7 A/157 BRAY	Fired 22 rounds A.X. registered A.7.b.2.9½. J.72.a.6.5½. A.8.8.4½.6. 6.10pm Fired 5 rounds A.X. into MAMETZ in retaliation.	

Army Form C. 2118.

WAR DIARY
or
INTELLIGENCE SUMMARY.

(Erase heading not required.)

Instructions regarding War Diaries and Intelligence Summaries are contained in F.S. Regs., Part II and the Staff Manual respectively. Title pages will be prepared in manuscript.

Hour, Date, Place	Summary of Events and Information	Remarks and references to Appendices
A/157 3/7/16 continued.	At 6 pm. Enemy 4.2 Hows. Battery fired about 16 rounds at A13d.1/o.6. B.9.1.1 in Carnoy.	
B/157 3/7/16	Registered target A11 A8 & A10a.6.4. Firing in all 11 rounds P.X. Reconstruction work carried on during the whole day. Quiet night. At 12 noon fired 5 rounds P.X. at Battery X16 a.4.7. which was firing towards ALBERT.	
C/157 3/7/16	At 6.30 am German 15dr. Battery 12 rounds at French 66. A great deal of traffic was noticed on CONTALMAISON-BAZENTIN ROAD, mounted troops wagons.	

WAR DIARY
or
INTELLIGENCE SUMMARY.

(Erase heading not required.)

Army Form C. 2118.

Hour, Date, Place	Summary of Events and Information	Remarks and references to Appendices
3/2/16 BRAY	Information received on this date that one battery of the Brigade was to be transferred to 51st. DIVISION. C Battery was selected. Transfer to be completed by 7th Feby, 1916.	Officers C/157 Lieut C.C. Welsh RFA Capt A.T.S. Napier RFA 2nd Lieut C. Holbury RFA 2nd Lt P. White
3/3/16 D/157 SUZANNE	Quiet. Fired 7 Rounds Registering.	
4/3/16 B/157 SUZANNE	Fired 25 Rds BY at A.17 D.1.6 on order of O/C Right Group. A large number of no 100 fuze 107 failing to burst. Fired 16 Rounds BY into HARDICOURT. One section of C/151 LEFT Battery returned action of C/151 GROUP.	
4/3/16 C/151 BRAY	Came out of action & bivouaced at Bayon Wood. Relieved by B/151.	

WAR DIARY
or
INTELLIGENCE SUMMARY.

(Erase heading not required.)

Army Form C. 2118.

Hour, Date, Place	Summary of Events and Information	Remarks and references to Appendices
D/151. 4.7.16 SUZANNE	Registered various points. Pamaterre E.Shot. Clo 100 Inf. Regt. Reine. Two men injured one Battery/R.F.A., also 6 men of 19 Siege Battery/R.G.A. on strength of D*. ENEMY Gas, Sausages up all day. Nothing to report. Quiet night.	
A/151. 5/151.	" Reconstruction work.	
D/151. SUZANNE	Enemy batteries up at ① MARICOURT. ② behind HERBICOURT. ③ BOIS de MEREAUCOURT. Fired 40 rounds in MEREAUCOURT & BOIS de MEREAUCOURT. Trenches at BOIS de MEREAUCOURT. A series of quick salvoes from two or three Enemy Batteries here fired at the Battery way into the shell fell into of Very Battery.	

WAR DIARY
or
INTELLIGENCE SUMMARY.

Army Form C. 2118.

(Erase heading not required.)

Hour, Date, Place	Summary of Events and Information	Remarks and references to Appendices
D/157 Continued. 5/7/16	Action. Two men killed and five wounded - 2 badly. Six men killed in the Siege Battery. Guns undamaged.	
157 B.A.C. 6/7/16	R.A.1 that portion of B.A.C. (personnel) not accompanying transferred to 51st DIVISION/ Fired 40 rounds BX into MONTAUBAN as ordered by Centre Group.	Both wagons 9/157
A/157 7/7/16	Fired to North BX into enemy battery position A.6.B.8.1. 3 Rounds battery keys since been silent to fire from valley in which enemy battery was situated. 16.30 BX fired in reply to our searching for batteries.	
B/157		

WAR DIARY
or
INTELLIGENCE SUMMARY.
(Erase heading not required.)

Army Form C. 2118.

Hour, Date, Place	Summary of Events and Information	Remarks and references to Appendices
6.76 SECTION D/157 Left Group. D/15/ 6.76	to be located somewhere near the north end of the FAVIERE WOOD. Considerable amount of traffic noticed along the COMBLES — GUILLEMONT ROAD. Fired 7 Rounds MX into MAMETZ in retaliation for shelling of CARNOY. Heavy firing by enemy on VAUX WOOD and THIEPVAL VILLAGE. From direction of THEM enemy fired on crest of VAUX WOOD. (y. 2 April) Battery firing HE and Shrapnel mostly Sheet 1.	
6.76 BRAY.	ENEMY dropped between 60 + 70 shells into BRAY, one striking a file	

WAR DIARY or INTELLIGENCE SUMMARY

Army Form C. 2118.

Hour, Date, Place	Summary of Events and Information	Remarks and references to Appendices
7.2/76. 17/157	at the Bus in the Brigade Adagio Garden. Very little Enemy firing beyond the Bee being destroyed, + whereon in respect of Bees onwards. Quiet since 7 p.m. previous day. Between 3 - 4.30 pm fired 68 rounds PK support towards our trenches in FIR a advanced of Infantry. Enemy barrage up.	Lieut 6. C. Hackett reported from 1st Reserve Bde Newcastle on Tyne. Posted to B/157
B/157	10 Rounds PK fired into HARDE-COURT on instructions from Right Group. Enemy 5.9 battery shelled the valley in which this battery is situated 6.15 p.m.	
D/157	Enemy shelled VAUX + VAUX WOOD quiet on Sector 1 + 2. Fired 16 rounds PK into CURLU.	

WAR DIARY
or
INTELLIGENCE SUMMARY.
(Erase heading not required.)

Army Form C. 2118.

Hour, Date, Place	Summary of Events and Information	Remarks and references to Appendices
8/76 9/15	This Battery was on this day transferred to 51st DIVISION, by/from with Captain by R.A.C. The following officers, other ranks were transferred, and material. Capt. R.F.S. Rogers. RFA. Lieut. O.C. WELSH. RFA. Lieut. C.E. ROBINSON. RFA. Lieut. H. WHITE. RFA. 132 Other ranks plus 2 A.T.C. personnel + 1 R.A.M.C. water duty man 4. 4. 5. Horse. with 8. Wagons Limbers (£32 nb) 1 Cycle Cart DR) 1 Water Cart 126 Horses.	

WAR DIARY
or
INTELLIGENCE SUMMARY.
(Erase heading not required.)

Hour, Date, Place	Summary of Events and Information	Remarks and references to Appendices
8/76 (Continued)	B/C. Hy. hostile (containing A.19.2 round Bn.), 626 N.E.° enemy/+ 3.2. forces.	
A/157.	Quiet. nothing to report.	
B/157	From reports received at SURVEY O.P. located Battery in the western portion of A.19.A. B/C searched the found in that vicinity but could ascertain no information as to results beyond the fact that enemy battery ceased firing. 12 rds B.X./ fired. Destruction work carried on. Enemy balloons up.	
D/157	Lippe/doning/ registered wood in square G.5.B.d.4.	

Hour, Date, Place	Summary of Events and Information	Remarks and references to Appendices
9.70. 17/1/57.	Very quiet. Registered a little.	
18/1/57.	At 10. a.m. Enemy 5·9 battery shelled road east of [D/157 pit chair?] presumably looking for 18 pdrs. Battery nearby. Two presumably badly [laid?] rounds fell into battery position, one burrowing B/c/o hut the other, a 'dud' entering one of the [men's?] dug outs. Day spent in repairs to telephone lines, and reconstruction work + Towards evening the Battery had a premature [?]. No. 700 fuze, No. [?] fuse (5th charge). No damage done.	

WAR DIARY
or
INTELLIGENCE SUMMARY.
(Erase heading not required.)

Army Form C. 2118.

Instructions regarding War Diaries and Intelligence Summaries are contained in F.S. Regs., Part II and the Staff Manual respectively. Title pages will be prepared in manuscript.

Hour, Date, Place	Summary of Events and Information	Remarks and references to Appendices
9 2/6 D/157.	Enemy shelled VAUX WOOD, otherwise very quiet all day. Fired 18 rounds AX at dritest in CURLU, effective.	
10 2/6 A/157	Between 12.15 am - 1.30 am Fired 20 rounds AX on second line trenches in B 3 at regiment of Infantry/1 and 10 rounds into MAMETZ. At 4.15 pm fired in retaliation 15 rds AX into MAMETZ, 8 round AX on A 9 a 1.9 and A 9 a 3.9 at regiment of Infantry/1. Otherwise quiet.	Lieut GA Hirkson rejoint from 31st Div. Bde RMA reported for duty from 7/D/151 to 7/D/151
B/157	Communication Trench A o.c. 7.7.5 dicad under orders of Right Group > 2 Bt Lt Lt HARDECOURT Right Group 6.40 pm	

Army Form C. 2118.

WAR DIARY
or
INTELLIGENCE SUMMARY.
(Erase heading not required.)

Instructions regarding War Diaries and Intelligence Summaries are contained in F.S. Regs., Part II and the Staff Manual respectively. Title pages will be prepared in manuscript.

Hour, Date, Place		Summary of Events and Information	Remarks and references to Appendices
10/9/16	D/157.	Very quiet day, spent in registration/work.	
11/9/16	A/157.	Very quiet, nothing to report.	
"	B/157	Fired 24 Rds RX into communication trench A.10.c.6.6. to A.10.c.6.8. in accordance with instructions received from OC Right group.	
"	D/157	Nil report.	
12/9/16	A/157. B/157 D/	Nothing to report, very quiet. B/157 report that a screen of gaffer hedge has been erected by enemy on COMBLES — GUILLEMONT ROAD. Traffic very heavy along this road. Screen evidently meant to hide same.	

(73989) W4141—463. 400,000. 9/14. H.&J.Ltd. Forms/C. 2118/10.

WAR DIARY
or
INTELLIGENCE SUMMARY.
(Erase heading not required.)

Army Form C. 2118.

Hour, Date, Place		Summary of Events and Information	Remarks and references to Appendices
13/7/16	A/157	Fired 3 rounds B.X on F.11.C.4 & 2 & F.11.6.8 at request of 74 DIVISION, who are on left of this Battery's position. Also fired 8 rounds at MAMETZ and 5 rounds on trenches opposite Trench 60.	
	B/157	8 rounds expended in testing/register. & 20 rounds B.X. fired into HARDECOURT. otherwise quiet.	
	D/157.	Observation difficult owing to mist. VAUX WOOD shelled by enemy from direction of HEM. Enemy followed immediate vicinity of Battery. No casualties. Captain F. Day Rifles. O/C D/157 in his daily report states:- "I saw Col. Fisher of 18th Manchesters Leavening/arranged	

WAR DIARY
or
INTELLIGENCE SUMMARY.
(Erase heading not required.)

Army Form C. 2118.

Hour, Date, Place	Summary of Events and Information	Remarks and references to Appendices
13/9/16 D/157 (continued)	"A" Light favourable to fire on a billet at CURLU at 6.30 a.m. 14th.	
14 9/10 A/157	Fired in retaliation on enemy trenches in F.12.a (5 Rds) Enemy working party on CARNOY – MONTAUBAN ROAD, fired 5 rounds 18x at same, grouping of timber blown out of a dug-out. Enemy shelled the whole length of PEROHNE AVENUE from CARNOY ROAD to CULVERT, direction of this battery appeared to be towards BRIQUETERIE. LATER The battery referred to above (a 77 mm) appears to be pouring shorts to be near BRIQUETERIE. Nothing to report.	
B/157		

WAR DIARY
or
INTELLIGENCE SUMMARY.
(Erase heading not required.)

Army Form C. 2118.

Hour, Date, Place	Summary of Events and Information	Remarks and references to Appendices
4.9/16 D/167.	As arranged yesterday with General Tower of 18th/MANCHESTERS fired 16 rounds into Billet 692 CVRLD. Later – 2pm. fired at Billet 692 reported to above, man finished to the dirt, out ran down the street. Fired again, shot caused rifle on turret man came running out. Two Offrs came out of a house near by ran to granny near Church. One Offrn copped up a field took photograph facing direction from which shells that came, then ran an inundiaf Kodak as he went. Fired 46 rounds into edge of wood searching round spot where	

Army Form C. 2118.

WAR DIARY
or
INTELLIGENCE SUMMARY.
(Erase heading not required.)

Instructions regarding War Diaries and Intelligence Summaries are contained in F.S. Regs., Part II and the Staff Manual respectively. Title pages will be prepared in manuscript.

Hour, Date, Place	Summary of Events and Information	Remarks and references to Appendices
14/7/6 D/157	machine guns are supposed to be placed	
15/7/6 A/157 B/157 D/	Very little doing, a few rounds fired by the batteries registering. Vicinity of D. being shelled by enemy	
16/7/6 A.B.+D. /157	Raining heavily, observation much hindered. Nothing of importance to report.	
17/7/6 "	Same as yesterday.	
18/7/6 "	Very little to report, day spent in reconstruction work.	
19/7/6 A/157 B/157	Fired a few rounds registering. Engaged machine gun emplacement	

Army Form C. 2118.

WAR DIARY
or
INTELLIGENCE SUMMARY.
(Erase heading not required.)

Instructions regarding War Diaries and Intelligence Summaries are contained in F.S. Regs., Part II. and the Staff Manual respectively. Title pages will be prepared in manuscript.

Hour, Date, Place		Summary of Events and Information	Remarks and references to Appendices
2/10	B/157	at A.17.D.3.7. 15 rounds BX fired in all.	
	D/157	Quiet, nothing to report	
20 3/10	A/157	A very bright day. German aeroplane flew over our communication trenches	
	B/157	Registered aforesaid enemy O.P. At 28.o.7½-7 firing 6 rounds BX.	
	D/157	11.35 am. fired at 2 machine gun emplacements below Chateau (30 rounds BX) 9 duds (fuzes 44) F.O.O. reported destruction of emplacements.	
21 3/10	A/157	Very wet. Some wind. Nothing to report. 1 Section of the Battery relieved	

WAR DIARY
or
INTELLIGENCE SUMMARY.
(Erase heading not required.)

Army Form C. 2118.

Hour, Date, Place	Summary of Events and Information	Remarks and references to Appendices
20/7/16 A/157	By a section of "C" Hoy Battery R.F.A. (57th DIVISION) (Coly C/157). The section relieved moved to rest billets at BUSSY LES DAOURS.	
21/7/16 B/157	Reconstruction work carried on, a very quiet day.	
" D/157	Day not very quiet. Right Section of this Battery relieved by Section of 2nd (Renfrewshire Battery) 1/2 (Highland) Bde R.F.A. (51st) DIVISION. Relieved section moved to rest billets at BUSSY LES DAOURS.	
22/7/16 A/157	11.15am Fired 5 rounds BX at 12a point 1368. Enemy fired 3 rounds heavy H.E. AGE towards CARNOY village in direction of BRONFAY FARM. Shrapnel burst in direction.	

WAR DIARY
or
INTELLIGENCE SUMMARY.

Army Form C. 2118.

Hour, Date, Place	Summary of Events and Information	Remarks and references to Appendices
22/7/16 B/157	10.15 am Opened searching fire on enemy's artillery working in B. 19.C. Fired 10 rounds on sheep position at 2.50 pm — firing in all 28 rounds BX. Registered various points.	Section of B/157 relieved By/ Section of 117 Highland (H) Howitzer Battery moved to BUSSY LES DAOURS.
23/7/16 D/157. A/157. B/157.	Very little to report. Gs D/157 fired 50 rounds on to several hostile targets for information of Howitzer Battery Commander who is registering Ring.	
24/7/16 HQ/157.	Very quiet. D. Battery. Instructions received this morning from HQ RA for D/157	

WAR DIARY
or
INTELLIGENCE SUMMARY.
(Erase heading not required.)

Army Form C. 2118.

Hour, Date, Place	Summary of Events and Information	Remarks and references to Appendices
24/7/16 D/157	To relieve 65th Battery RFA. (8th Bde) who were going out this evening. To carry this out the detachment of B & D/157 not at Bruay will come up & the one bringing with them the guns of Oct 7/9th Hyfields. D&DMA which they took over. Later 65th Battery came out of action about 1 am & D Battery took over their position, using the guns mentioned above. The fed position of D/157 was thus under the command of Capt Walker, 1/3rd Kept Land Bde, B personnel being in action at his own battery in a section of B/157.	

WAR DIARY
or
INTELLIGENCE SUMMARY.
(Erase heading not required.)

Army Form C. 2118.

Hour, Date, Place	Summary of Events and Information	Remarks and references to Appendices
25/2/16. BRAY.	Snowing. Observation difficult.	
26/2/16 A/157.	Left section carried out action at 10 am, being relieved by C/157 RFA at 7/3rd Highland How Bde RFA, moved to Pot Biets at BUSSY.	
26/2/16 B/157 & Hdqrs 157	Relieved by 2nd Reserve Battery 1/3rd Highland Bde. Relieved by Headquarters 1/3rd Highland How Bde.	
27/2/16 157/BAC	2 Sections of the column relieved by Column of 1/3rd Highland Brigade RFA. 1 Section under Lieut J.P. Boyd left behind to supply ammunition to D/157. Instructions received at 11.30pm	

Army Form C. 2118.

WAR DIARY
or
INTELLIGENCE SUMMARY.
(Erase heading not required.)

Hour, Date, Place	Summary of Events and Information	Remarks and references to Appendices
28/7/16	For the Bde to return to the line & take up old position on 28th inst thus relieving 1/7th Highland Bde R.F.A. and thereafter.	
29/7/16 A & B /157	Brigade returned to the line. Reconstructing positions & generally surveying the ground in their zone for arty perspective arcs coming (but I establish or 25 & 26 inst respectively) Very quiet, nothing of interest to report.	
D/157		
29/7/16		

Ayer
Lieut Col RA
Comdg. 157. Arty.

151 - RFA 4

WAR DIARY
or
INTELLIGENCE SUMMARY.
(Erase heading not required.)

Army Form C. 2118.

Hour, Date, Place		Summary of Events and Information	Remarks and references to Appendices

1/3/16. D. 11 A.m. Fired 3 Rds. Bx on A 8 8. 9
Between 10.30 + 11 A.m. & 4.2 How fired about 6 rds on a
working party at F.23.6.9.0. 77 M.M. fired 6 rds on emplacement
This failing stopped all work for the day in this locality.

9.30 A.m. German working party fired on the French going
POMMIERS Dpt A.2.c.2.4

B. Day spent in reconstruction work + repair of
telephone wires

D.
9.45 A.m. Fired 6 rds along road by True Hill as usual
11.0 A.m. Fired on new work under Bernie Rd, observed many
duds. Partial demolition probably owing to
soil being very strong + very stiff.

2/3/16. A/151. Quiet day. Nothing to report.

B/151. Fired 8 rounds into trench A 23
8.40 a.m. B.0.3 in accordance with instructions

WAR DIARY
or
INTELLIGENCE SUMMARY.
(Erase heading not required.)

Army Form C. 2118.

Hour, Date, Place	Summary of Events and Information	Remarks and references to Appendices
B/157 2/1/0 (Continues) 11.30	Received from O/C., Centre Group R.A. Intimated up to 2pm fired 56 rounds P.X. searching for enemy Battery/ fired 24 rounds B.X/ adjusted on communication trenches B79. A.	
D/157 12.15pm	Officer & somewhere seen in Ellet A 30.c. 63. (curld), firing 10 B.X. 1.6. being "dud". Later 40 R.X. fired into Sap under PERONNE ROAD, very satisfactory/ and abandoned. Enemy 4.2 Battery fired 6 rounds	
5.10pm	H.E. into VAUX WOOD.	

WAR DIARY
or
INTELLIGENCE SUMMARY.

(Erase heading not required.)

Army Form C. 2118.

Hour, Date, Place	Summary of Events and Information	Remarks and references to Appendices
3.30 A/157	Quiet. No firing by this Battery during the day.	
	At 9.30 am enemy 77mm battery fired 3 rounds in direction of BILLON WOOD. Repeated at 9.45 am.	
B/157	At 3.30 pm enemy 4.2 battery in S.29.A.8.1. observed firing on our trenches 27-28. Searched for also. Battery firing 20 rounds B.R. at the values trench fired 24 rounds BX at communication trench A.11.C.7.3.	
5.15 pm	Fired 12 rounds BX on front line trench in A.10.D. as ordered by O/C Centre Group.	

WAR DIARY
or
INTELLIGENCE SUMMARY.
(Erase heading not required.)

Army Form C. 2118.

Hour, Date, Place	Summary of Events and Information	Remarks and references to Appendices
3. 3/16. D/157	Very quiet day.	
12.30 pm	Saw smoke of shell rising from trench leading down to CHAPEAU DE GENDARME A 29 D 7½ 8.	
5 pm	Enemy battery fired 14 rounds HE (4.2) into VAUX WOOD. In retaliation fired 12 rounds BX into Y WOOD.	
4. 3/16 A/157 B/157 D/157	Observation difficult all day. Inclement weather. SNOW.	
	ENEMY batteries very quiet. 9 rounds from 4/B battery fired into VAUX WOOD during day.	
5. 3/16 A/157	Fired 1K rounds BX. registered points.	
At 2.45 pm	Enemy 77. mm. Battery	

WAR DIARY
or
INTELLIGENCE SUMMARY.
(Erase heading not required.)

Army Form C. 2118.

Hour, Date, Place	Summary of Events and Information	Remarks and references to Appendices
A/157 5/9/16 (Continued)	Fired several rounds shrapnel on PERONNE ROAD in direction of Culvert.	
3.45 pm	Enemy 4.2 How Battery fired 2 rounds in direction of F.28.a.	
4.40 pm	Same Battery fired several rounds about the gallent on PERONNE ROAD & at 5.30 pm several rounds fired into LUCKNOW AVENUE and Grounds in F.28.c.	
B/157	Checked registration on point A.17.a 8/2. 3 rifle line trench 6.7 px expended.	
D/157 9 am	Machine gun fired from direction of CAPEAU DE GENDARME.	

WAR DIARY
or
INTELLIGENCE SUMMARY.
(Erase heading not required.)

Army Form C. 2118.

Hour. Date. Place	Summary of Events and Information	Remarks and references to Appendices
D/157 (Continued)	Made enquiries respecting groups of enemy infantry seen in trench @ 18.B.4.9.	
10. am	Machine gun fire opened.	
10.45am	Enemy fired 5 rounds (from HEM) fired 2 rounds into LODGE WOOD	
1.30 pm	Enemy 4.2 Battery fired from direction of HEM WOOD 10 rounds very slow fire on to WELL HEAD structure near schoolhouse G 10.c.8.3.	
3.5 pm 3.15 pm	28 Rounds 4.2 HE fired into DRAGONS WOOD.	
6 3/16 A/151 B/151 D/151	A very quiet day. Nothing to report.	

Army Form C. 2118.

WAR DIARY
or
INTELLIGENCE SUMMARY.
(Erase heading not required.)

Instructions regarding War Diaries and Intelligence Summaries are contained in F.S. Regs., Part II and the Staff Manual respectively. Title pages will be prepared in manuscript.

Hour, Date, Place	Summary of Events and Information	Remarks and references to Appendices
3/10 7 A/157	Fired 17 rounds DPX registered A 30.9.5 v A 3c. 05b0. Enemy fired several rounds (77mm) on our Communication trenches in line about A 19 B.	
5.50 pm	Several rounds , 4.2 How fired at BRONFAY FARM, F 29.B. 2 Direct hits	
B/157.	Battery employed on constructing new gun pits. Fired 3 rounds D/6 Gun, object on A 17 B. 1.9 ½.	
D/157	Enemy shelled VAUX VILLAGE – about 6 k.g. rounds 5.15 pm fired 18 rounds HE into CURLU in retaliation for enemy shelling of VAUX WOOD.	

Army Form C. 2118.

WAR DIARY
or
INTELLIGENCE SUMMARY.
(Erase heading not required.)

Instructions regarding War Diaries and Intelligence Summaries are contained in F.S. Regs., Part II. and the Staff Manual respectively. Title pages will be prepared in manuscript.

Hour, Date, Place	Summary of Events and Information	Remarks and references to Appendices
8/3/16 A/151	1 pm. Fired 14 rounds on loophole at point F 6 c 8.0. and on trench in A 3 a 4.7. 4. pm. Enemy to stop Battery fired 9 rounds in directions BR6N BAY FARM At 8.30 am 2 men were seen to enter the ruins of the MILL at S 27 c 4.2. a booked epitaph noise arose, but the ruins were closely watched. Nothing to report.	
B/151		
D/151 1.30 pm	Fired 31 rounds Box on to SMID BAG TRENCH. Nothing particular to record.	
9/3/16 to 10/3/16	Observation officers out to enemy towing.	
11/3/16 A/B/D/151	Nothing to report.	

WAR DIARY
or
INTELLIGENCE SUMMARY.

Army Form C. 2118.

Hour, Date, Place	Summary of Events and Information	Remarks and references to Appendices
12/10 A/51	Misty morning. Registered two new targets.	
B/51	Fired 29 rounds AX in searching for Enemy's Battery in B.7.D.5.8. (approximate)	
C/51	Tested registration of various points. Nothing unusual — fairly quiet.	
D/51		
13/10 A/51	Registered new target. Shick of two mines during following up during night. Day wet.	
B/51	Fired 26 AX on A.10.D.8.7 in accordance with instructions at 9.45 am.	
D/51	Quiet day.	

WAR DIARY
or
INTELLIGENCE SUMMARY.
(Erase heading not required.)

Army Form C. 2118.

Hour, Date, Place	Summary of Events and Information	Remarks and references to Appendices
14/3/16	Nothing to record.	
15/3/16 - 20/3/16	Very little activity. Sniper firing at our front, slackening/registers worthy.	
22/3/16	Headquarters, Brigade moved out of BRAY to BUSSY. Battalion left in billets. 18th DIVISION took over from 30th	
28/3/16	Headquarters, Brigade moved to St SAVEUR.	
	Clayton Lieut Col R7H Comdg 1st A[rty]	

RFA 151 Vol S
Army Form C. 2118.

30 Div

WAR DIARY
or
INTELLIGENCE SUMMARY.
(Erase heading not required.)

Hour, Date, Place	Summary of Events and Information	Remarks and references to Appendices
April 1916 A, B & J/151	Our fire About 50 rounds per week expended by each Battery chiefly in retaliation at request of Groups one or two rounds intensive fire on to selected spots such as Montauban, Bernafay Wood, Chapeau de Gendarme, & Y Wood. On these occasions a rate of fire of 5 to 6 rounds per gun per minute was usually obtained	
26/4/16	A" Battery put one gun forward in a position due east of Carnoy & about 50 yds N.W. of Copse. On the night of the 28-29 a report fire of 10 mins duration was poured on A9.b.2.6 with the principal object of cutting the enemy's wire. 52nd	

WAR DIARY
or
INTELLIGENCE SUMMARY.
(Erase heading not required.)

Army Form C. 2118.

Instructions regarding War Diaries and Intelligence Summaries are contained in F. S. Regs., Part II and the Staff Manual respectively. Title pages will be prepared in manuscript.

Hour, Date, Place	Summary of Events and Information	Remarks and references to Appendices
28/4/16 A/151 April 1916	4 H.E. were fired in the 10 mm. The other 3 guns fired in conjunction with the Battery put up a barrage round the Copse & fired live trench at the spot for 20 mins while the infantry went over & destroyed the enemy works. One shrapnel the following day the enemy were seen in a group of about 10 or 15 yds apart & at once away. <u>Hostile fire</u> Received intense bursts on different localities such as Vance Village & Billow Wood & Counter Battery work on Stewcourt Valley. Very little further shelling. Principally 15 c.m. & 77 m.m. shell were fired during the events.	

WAR DIARY
or
INTELLIGENCE SUMMARY.
(Erase heading not required.)

Army Form C. 2118.

Hour, Date, Place	Summary of Events and Information	Remarks and references to Appendices
April 1916. A.B. & J/15.1	**Enemy movement** Very little movement observed. Road convoy disgorged as unusual were seen during trench work in Curlu village. Train Service Rly-Service Normal Transport Normal Observation Balloons & Aeroplanes Owing to the high winds prevalent during the month of April there was much less activity than during the previous month **Brigade** assumed command here on the 10th April 1916	

Army Form C. 2118.

WAR DIARY
or
INTELLIGENCE SUMMARY.
(Erase heading not required.)

Instructions regarding War Diaries and Intelligence Summaries are contained in F. S. Regs., Part II and the Staff Manual respectively. Title pages will be prepared in manuscript.

Hour, Date, Place	Summary of Events and Information	Remarks and references to Appendices
A, B, & D Batteries 151st Bde.	Work done by Battery	
April 1916.	Very extensive wiring & defensive work about Chapter Wood. New work has also been done at Tom Turpost & at Pommier redoubt. Work done by new Batteries are	
A/151	New O.P. completed, Ammunition completed	
D/151	Gun position built for 4 Guns	
B/151	Position strengthened & tunnels between Guns & dug-outs cut	

C. Ayer Lt Col RA
Comdg 151/Bde

RFA 151406
158 Bde
30th Div

WAR DIARY
or
INTELLIGENCE SUMMARY.

Army Form C. 2118.

Hour, Date, Place	Summary of Events and Information	Remarks and references to Appendices
May 1916 A 2/5/16	Exchanged positions with C. Battery 85th Bde. taking over their Guns & Ammunition in 120 Wilhemite Road. East of Auzanne.	
	Not much firing done, as this Battery was on the extreme right of the British line, work was done in conjunction with the French, called upon twice to put a barage on our right twice to hood and a Minnewerfer in enemys front line trench	
12/5/16	Launched & New Gun pits at the rest Sacing east of Wilhemite Road, also new dugouts at the West, the work had been started by one Predicissins & the position was well chosen & very strongly built.	
	One Section moved in on the night of the 10th May & the other on the night of the 11th.	

WAR DIARY
or
INTELLIGENCE SUMMARY.
(Erase heading not required.)

Army Form C. 2118.

Hour, Date, Place	Summary of Events and Information	Remarks and references to Appendices
15/5/16. "A"	Ordered to build a new position about 700 yds due North of MARICOURT and work was started at once under cover of a screen, notwithstanding the enemy balloon must have observed work going on as the position was shelled by 15 C.M. + 77 M.M. guns on May 18th. There were no casualties. Lieut J.G. Statham left the Battery to take up position of Adjutant.	
21/5/16	Owing to a reorganization scheme the 151st (C.P.) Field Bde. was taken up & this Battery became "D" 134, 148 Bde from this date	
"B"	A very quiet month on the whole, with practical activity on the part of the enemy towards. Various work improving strengthing our position	

WAR DIARY
or
INTELLIGENCE SUMMARY.
(Erase heading not required.)

Army Form C. 2118.

Hour, Date, Place	Summary of Events and Information	Remarks and references to Appendices
May/1916 B/151	Reorganisation completed	
21/5/16	On the reorganisation of Artillery coming into effect this Battery became "D" Battery 169th Bde.	
"D"	Enemy has steadily diminished from the 1st to 21st. Very little back area shelled.	
	Movement	
	On 6 "show" twice hundred Clay Street. After the first shoot the trail came more Ypres for 3 days & since the 2nd shoot on the 15th and no trains have been seen when entering or leaving Horse transport normal. Large relief of Infantry with 100 Wagons marched in & out of Reninck on 15/5/16.	

WAR DIARY
or
INTELLIGENCE SUMMARY.

Army Form C. 2118.

Hour, Date, Place		Summary of Events and Information	Remarks and references to Appendices
11/5/16	D	On the night 11-12 May the Last Gun was moved into the New pits. The guns were all registered & the pits proved quite satisfactory. Enemy shelled the Valley rather heavily on two nights most of the Shell fell near the Battery Dig-out.	
21/5/16		The Battery, owing to the re-organization of the Artillery became "D" Battery 150 Bde. The Brigade Ammn Column was also broken up at this date. Some of the personnel & horses were transferred to A, B & D Batteries to bring them up to establishment & a number voluntarily for T.M. including Capt the Hon. G.H. Edwards & Lieut. J.P. Patterson who were also transferred to T.M. Batteries.	25/5/16 Major RFA 151/ASy

151st Bde R.F.A. 30th Division.

151 RFA
Army Fortfeeure ?
Vol. 7

WAR DIARY
or
INTELLIGENCE SUMMARY.
(Erase heading not required.)

Instructions regarding War Diaries and Intelligence Summaries are contained in F.S. Regs., Part II and the Staff Manual respectively. Title pages will be prepared in manuscript.

Hour, Date, Place	Summary of Events and Information	Remarks and references to Appendices
BOIS-DES-TAILLES 21/5/16	Owing to a re-organisation of the Artillery the following 18 pr Batteries were posted to this Brigade D/148, D/149, D/150 & manned A, B, & C 151 Bde respectively. At this batteries were in action in the right of the Bihut vac.	
A/151	Battery of neither to spent, not little pining done. All spare men employed in building a new position in the S.E. corner of BILLON WOOD	
B/151 4.15 P.M.	Fired 300 AX at Dump in trench. Fire direct on. Particularly occupied.	
11 P.M.	Enemy retaliated with about 100 10.5 CM & 77 M.M. Firing inflicted upon our customs. No casualties were sustained.	

(73989) W4141—463. 400,000. 9/14. H.&J.Ltd. Forms/C. 2118/10.

157th Bde RFA. 30th Division

WAR DIARY
of
INTELLIGENCE SUMMARY.
(Erase heading not required.)

Army Form C. 2118.

Hour, Date, Place	Summary of Events and Information	Remarks and references to Appendices
13/1/51		
25/5/16	Large movement of enemy forces of all branches were observed on the road leading into Cleg/Obere and Mont St Quentin. Four Companies were seen marching to the rear & left of Cleg. They started their trucks & removed about 10 different formations. Nothing could be seen nothing early the following morning about 3 Companies again appeared on the R. Cleg. They received two enemy trucks.	
9.45 to 10.15 PM 25/5/16	Enemy fired 99 4.2 shells in the valley near to the battery position. 53 duds were counted.	
11.15 to 11.20 P.M	60 more 4.2 shells fell near the Battery position. Most of them suffered short & no damage was done. They appeared to come from the direction of Battery Copse.	

1st S. Bde R.F.A. 30th Division

Army Form C. 2118.

WAR DIARY
or
INTELLIGENCE SUMMARY.

(Erase heading not required.)

Instructions regarding War Diaries and Intelligence Summaries are contained in F.S. Regs., Part II. and the Staff Manual respectively. Title pages will be prepared in manuscript.

Hour, Date, Place	Summary of Events and Information	Remarks and references to Appendices
B/151 27/5/16 10.15 p.m.	About 60 5.9 shells dropped in the valley near our position. No damage was done.	
28/5/16	A good deal of fire at Fontaine Wood & at A machine gun emplacement in Chapeau H. at an O.P. in Bernafay Wood.	
29/5/16	Enemy fired into Trench Pat & VAUX WOOD	
30/5/16	Fired on Machine Gun which was active on Maltz Horn Farm. Retaining fire	
31/5/16	Fired Corral rounds at LA GRENOUILLERE & 4 TREE POST. Fired our barrage east to cover the FRENCH the change & bombed out the Faux foundry.	
6/151 21/9 pm	MARICOURT VALLEY shelled intermittently from 9 to 10.30 P.M. heavily shelled from 11 p.m. - 5 A.M.	

151st Bde R.F.A. 30th Division

WAR DIARY
or
INTELLIGENCE SUMMARY.

Hour, Date, Place	Summary of Events and Information	Remarks and references to Appendices
8/1/51	Enemy shelled MARICOURT VALLEY intermittently between	
25/5/16	9 + 11 pm	
26/5/16	Enemy shelled SUZANNE + South end of MARICOURT VALLEY between 8 + 10 AM	
28 + 29/5/16	Battery first shoot occurred each day in retaliation for shelling of our front line. Found established on our back area on Enemy's front line from A17a 2.9 to A17a 30.95	

Olyer Bre Wn.

151st Bde R.F.A. 30th Division

WAR DIARY
or
INTELLIGENCE SUMMARY
(Erase heading not required.)

Army Form C. 2118

Instructions regarding War Diaries and Intelligence Summaries are contained in F.S. Regs., Part II. and the Staff Manual respectively. Title Pages will be prepared in manuscript.

Place	Date	Hour	Summary of Events and Information	Remarks and references to Appendices
BOIS-DE-TAILLES	1/6/16		"A" Battery. Right Section emplacues from site knocken just East of SUZANNE & put into action with 4 guns of C/149 in Copse "S" covering FRISE CAUSEWAY & enfilading enemy trenches opposite the French on bank of river Somme. Left Section in action at VAUX WOOD covering MARICOURT	
R/151	14/6/16		All spare men building new gun position at S.E corner of BILLON WOOD	
			Left Section withdrawn from VAUX WOOD & sent down to Wagon Line at ETINEHEM. The Zeros having been handed over to the French.	
	10/6/16		Right section withdrawn from Copse "S" & sent to Wagon Line	
	7/6/16		Battery at work on New position & also helping to dig new position for the 9.2" Siemens behind BILLON WOOD & at OXFORD COPSE	
	21/6/16	10 P.M	Got guns into New position	
	22/6/16		Registered all Bench on allotted Zone	
	23/6/16		Bombardment started. Battery's task, to cut wire on GLATZ REDOUBT	
	24 & 30		& ALT TRENCH also to shell O.P's	
			Bombardment continued	
	1/7/16	7.30 AM	Infantry assaulted & took MONTAUBAN at 10.30 AM. This attack was	

1st Bde R.H.A. 30th 16 Division

Army Form C. 2118

WAR DIARY
or
INTELLIGENCE SUMMARY
(Erase heading not required.)

Place	Date	Hour	Summary of Events and Information	Remarks and references to Appendices
BOIS-AUX-TAILLES B/161	1/6/16	Various 12	Supported by our Artillery fire the whole day. Guns moved forward to a position at OXFORD COPSE. Inspection of enemy trenches found these to have been battered out of all recognition. Wire entanglements were entirely destroyed, while some entanglements were shelled between twenty & thirty yards from our lot.	
B/151	1/6/16 to 1/6/16	1.10PM to 1.50PM	SUZANNE & South end of MARICOURT VALLEY were shelled. One gun put one lot & all telephone wires were cut. So casualties	
	6/6/16		Battery moved forward to its new position about ½ mile S.W. of MARICOURT	
	8/6/16	P.M.	36 rounds were fired for registration of Gun Zone	
	12/6/16	11.35 to 12.50	Battery fired 379 rounds in response to a S.O.S call from Infantry. A few stray shells fell near the Battery but no damage was done	
	16/6/16	10.15 PM to 10 wm	40 rounds fired in retaliation at request of Infantry who were being worried by Trench Mortars. Result most effective.	
	19/6/16		36 rounds were fired for registration, with a view to future wire cutting	
	24/6/16	8-12 AM	About 400 rounds were fired to cut wire in front of enemy trenches	

151st Bde RFA 30th Division

WAR DIARY
or
INTELLIGENCE SUMMARY
(Erase heading not required.)

Army Form C. 2118

Instructions regarding War Diaries and Intelligence Summaries are contained in F.S. Regs., Part II. and the Staff Manual respectively. Title Pages will be prepared in manuscript.

Place	Date	Hour	Summary of Events and Information	Remarks and references to Appendices
12/151	25/6/16	12 noon 7 p.m.	Slow cutting continued about 800 rounds fired	
	26/6/16	8-12 4 p.m.	" " " 600 " "	
	27/6/16		Communication taken down. no firing done	
	28/6/16	12 noon 7 p.m.	Wire cutting continued about 100 rounds fired	
	29/6/16	10 to 12 noon	" " " 200 " "	
	30/6/16		All was apparently cut & a few rounds were fired between 2 & 3 p.m. to verify reported ranges on various points. Between June 7 & 19 the Battery were busily employed in completing the position occupied on June 3rd. A big lot of building material was carted up for this & also for a reserve position for the 9.2" Gun. About 6000 rounds of Ammunition were dumped at the Battery position. Nothing of interest to report. Engaged in & building New Gun position	

13/151

151st Bde R.F.A. 30th Division

Army Form C. 2118

WAR DIARY
or
INTELLIGENCE SUMMARY
(Erase heading not required.)

Place	Date	Hour	Summary of Events and Information	Remarks and references to Appendices
B/151	June/16		in the MARICOURT VALLEY. Wire cutting & general bombardment to prepare for Infantry assault from the 24th to 31st June. 2 Lieut T.J. WEISS died of Wounds received in action.	
	29/6/16			

Alyer Roe
O.C. 151st (Co. Palatine) Brigade R.F.A.

WAR DIARY or INTELLIGENCE SUMMARY

Army Form C/2118

July

151 A⁴ᵈ
30 Division

Vol 8

Place	Date	Hour	Summary of Events and Information	Remarks and references to Appendices
A/151 30 DIV. A⁴ᵈ	1/7/16		After one days preliminary wire cutting, the battery participated in the final bombardment prior to Infantry attack at 7.30 A.M. Battery moved forward into a position at Gospel Copse North of the PERONNE Rd. Fired more or less day & night. Harassing French approaches to MONTAUBAN VILLAGE & bombarding enemys Gun line.	
	10/15/7/16		During this period the Battery took part in three attacks on TRONES WOOD & aided to stop several counter attacks.	
	16/7/16	3 A.M.	Battery moved forward into position about 400 yds South of BRICQUETERIE on BRICQUETERIE — MARICOURT Rd. From this date to the end of the Month employed in replenishing when nothing on enemy's 2nd line GUILLEMONT VILLAGE and when working on the capture of DELVILLE WOOD FALFEMONT FARM, aided in the attack on GUILLEMONT on 27ᵗʰ & on the attack on GUILLEMONT on the latter & LOIGUEVAL on the 29ᵗʰ.	
	27/7/16		July 30ᵗʰ. the Battery was heavily shelled, especially during the afternoon part of the months. Major C.L.T WALWYN been wounded by shrapnel on the 21ˢᵗ Lieut E.C. BARBER was wounded while acting as F.O.O during operations on the 1st and for his services on that day he was awarded the MILITARY CROSS.	

Army Form C. 2118

WAR DIARY
or
INTELLIGENCE SUMMARY

(Erase heading not required.)

A/151.
30th Divisional Arty

Instructions regarding War Diaries and Intelligence Summaries are contained in F.S. Regs., Part II. and the Staff Manual respectively. Title Pages will be prepared in manuscript.

Place	Date	Hour	Summary of Events and Information	Remarks and references to Appendices
A/151	23/1/16 – 27/7/16	–	2/Lieut H.V. DANGAR & 2/Lieut S.S. EVANS were accidentally injured, the former breaking his ankle & the latter being thrown from his horse. Both these officers were evacuated.	
	2/7/16		2/Lieut T.H. BRINDLE-KELLY joined & 2/Lieut W.H. BLOOR & 2/Lieut E. PAYNE were attached for duty on the 27th.	
	19/7/16		2/Lieut W.H. WHEELER was posted to the battery & joined on this date. During the month the battery sustained the following casualties:– 4 Officers, 3 Sergts., 1 Corpl., 1 Bomb., 7 Gnrs & 1 Driver	
B/151	1/7/16	A.M. 6.25 to 7.30 A.M.	Directed on the intense bombardment of enemy's 1st line, support & communication trenches. Infantry took the narrow trenches BRIC_ue- Catin Trenches & Barrage was moved from time to time with few casualties & Barrage on enemy	
		P.M. 12.34	ETERIE was taken at 12.34 P.M.	
	2/7/16 to 3/7/16		Enemy shelled MONTAUBAN & BRIQVETERIE heavily. Battery fired on enemy 2nd line & on Barrage lines all night.	
	4/7/16		Assisted in attack on BERNAFAY WOOD which was taken at 2.15 P.M.	

Army Form C. 2118

WAR DIARY
or
INTELLIGENCE SUMMARY

(Erase heading not required.)

B/151st Brigade RFA
30th Divnl Arty

Instructions regarding War Diaries and Intelligence Summaries are contained in F.S. Regs., Part II. and the Staff Manual respectively. Title Pages will be prepared in manuscript.

Place	Date	Hour	Summary of Events and Information	Remarks and references to Appendices
PERONNE ROAD	6/7/16		Battery advanced & came into action just North of the PERONNE Rd. Registered guns on TRONES WOOD	
	7/7/16	P.M. 6.30	Ordered to move battery forward to take up a forward South of BRIQUETERIE to give one wire in front of TRONES WOOD. Owing to the terrible conditions & heavy rain was unable to go as far forward	
	8/7/16	A.M. 1.30	as desired. Stopped into action at 1.30 A.M. in old Bn Hqd land at about A10 c 3 3	
		7.30 A.M.	Started to cut wire in C.H. face of TRONES WOOD. Took infantry attack (Southern portion of Wood captured at 1 P.M. not successful. 2/Lieut F.W. HAEFFNER killed by enemy	
	9/7/16		MALTZ HORN FARM captured shell close to the Battery	
	10/7/16 to 11/7/16		Comparatively quiet days, started to cut 2nd line wire to North of GUILLEMONT. Enemy continues to shell TRONES WOOD heavily & launch counter attacks	
	13/7/16 to 17/7/16		Fairly quiet days. Enemy made several attempts to retake LONGUEVAL & DELVILLE WOOD. Battery called upon to barrage out from time to time	

B/15.1 A.A.
30th Division

WAR DIARY
or
INTELLIGENCE SUMMARY.

Army Form C. 2118.

(Erase heading not required.)

Hour, Date, Place	Summary of Events and Information	Remarks and references to Appendices
18 to 24th July 1916	Nothing of great importance on our immediate front. All time on most face of GUILLEMONT. Great difficulty in finding place to observe from.	
26/7/16	Battery heavily shelled with 10.5 & 15 c.m. shells. Had 2 Cpls & 4 men wounded. Wish to place on record the splendid work of Sgt. Cook who showed great courage whilst driving the wounded under heavy fire.	
27/7/16	Supported Infantry in attack on LONGUEVAL & DELVILLE WOOD which had been evacuated.	
28/7/16	Registered guns on important places in rear of enemy 2nd line system which later proved very useful. Count Potocki O.P. in French area. Learnt when the attack on GUILLEMONT could be seen.	
30/7/16 4.45 P.M.	Our Infantry attacked GUILLEMONT, fired on several barrages during the attack.	

WAR DIARY
or
INTELLIGENCE SUMMARY.
(Erase heading not required.)

Army Form C. 2118.

B/151 Bty
30th Division

Hour, Date, Place	Summary of Events and Information	Remarks and references to Appendices
30/7/16 11 AM	Large body of Germans seen retiring from FALFEMONT FARM & WEDGE WOOD. Turned battery on to them, doing great damage.	
11.30 AM	Enemy launched counter attack on GUILLEMONT from LEUZE-WOOD. Two batteries of the French 75 M.M batteries turned on to the enemy & two batteries together with other 18 pdrs had to attack over a mile of open ground. Attack stopped about 300 yds short of GUILLEMONT, what remained of the enemy had to retire through our fire. French batteries followed them and columns were sent by our troops, the great execution was done by our troops, the French fire being extremely rapid. Other good targets were observed during the & the following day & specially dealt with	
31/7/16		

WAR DIARY
or
INTELLIGENCE SUMMARY
(Erase heading not required.)

Army Form C. 2118

C/151 Arty
30th Division

Place	Date	Hour	Summary of Events and Information	Remarks and references to Appendices
C/151	1/7/16	AM 6.35	Assisted in final bombardment of Enemys front line trenches South of MONTAUBAN. Lifted barrage from there to keep as the Infantry took their objectives, finally putting up a barrage N.W. of the village	
	2/7/16	12 Noon	FREND went forward as F.O.O. to MONTAUBAN Fired almost continuously till 7 P.M. after that at irregular intervals throughout the night	
	2/7/16 & 3/7/16		Fired plenty on barrage lines, at irregular intervals	
	8/7/16		Moved forward to a position at OXFORD COPSE owing to bad state of ground the last guns did not arrive till 4 PM on the 9th.	
	9/7/16		Put up a barrage east of TRONES WOOD & twice during the day	
	10/9/16		the north end of the wood.	
	11/7/16	PM 3.27	Continued barrage on N.E. end of TRONES WOOD fired by map at our trenches near WATERLOT FARM Observation of this point impossible.	

WAR DIARY or INTELLIGENCE SUMMARY

Army Form C. 2118

B/151 Bty
30 Division

Place	Date	Hour	Summary of Events and Information	Remarks and references to Appendices
	12/7/16		Bombarded TRONES WOOD during evening. Two S.O.S. calls during the night	
	13/7/16	P.M. 2.45	Battery fired almost continuously since 2.45 P.M. till midnight	
		5 P.M.	Commenced on Northern half of TRONES WOOD. Intense bombardment began. Infantry entered the wood at 7 P.M. & finally captured it	
	14/7/16	3.20 A.M.	Barrage N.E. corner of TRONES WOOD, stopped firing about 7 A.M. Answered two S.O.S. calls between 10 P.M. & midnight	
	15/7/16	6 P.M.	Battery advanced to a position near DUBLIN TRENCH about out two on GUILLEMONT & came into action at 9 A.M. Wire cutting throughout the afternoon	
	16/7/16	2.53 A.M.	Fired on country N.E. of WATERLOT FARM towards GUILLEMONT where enemy were reported to be entrenching. Wire cutting at intervals during the rest of the day. One gun to CORBIE for repairs	
	17/7/16		Wire cutting. Heavy artillery very active. Before buffer trouble with two other guns which had to be withdrawn for repairs	

WAR DIARY or INTELLIGENCE SUMMARY

Army Form C. 2118

B/151 Bty
30th Division

Place	Date	Hour	Summary of Events and Information	Remarks and references to Appendices
B/151	18/7/16		Battery reduced to one gun. Tried our barrage line early morning, rest of day quiet	
	19/7/16		One gun returned & put back into position	
	20/7/16		Put up barrage in support of infantry attack on MALTZ HORN RIDGE. Attack not successful. Enemy artillery very active	
	21/7/16		4th gun returned & put into position, informed that the enemy gun was considered owing to wire & ditch near chamber. Fired 200 rounds for 4 wire cutting. Fired in support of infantry raid & later on enemy wire	
	22/7/16		Ammunition dumped by enemy fire during the afternoon	
	23/7/16	3.40 am	Supported infantry attack on GUILLEMONT, village strongly held. Our infantry reached the Church but all had to withdraw. Fired at intervals throughout the day till 6 P.M, afterwards a quiet night	

WAR DIARY or INTELLIGENCE SUMMARY

Army Form C. 2118

C/151 Bty
30th Division

Place	Date	Hour	Summary of Events and Information	Remarks and references to Appendices
C/151	24/7/16 to 26/7/16		Fired at irregular intervals at GUILLEMONT & approaches thereto with an occasional barrage N. of DELVILLE WOOD	
	27/7/16	7.10 AM	Fired salvoes at irregular intervals on wire & trenches S.W. of GUILLEMONT	
			Put up a barrage W. of GINCHY in support of Infantry attack N. of DELVILLE WOOD	
	28 & 29		Fired at irregular intervals on wire W. of GUILLEMONT each day. Enemy fired some heavy & incendiary shell into the valley in front of Battery position. Stopped firing about 8 P.M. A very disturbed night owing to shell fire between 10 & 11 P.M. & again between 2 & 3 A.M. of Battery position.	
	30/7/16	3.30 PM	all ranks were G.O. Reports "F.O.O" S/Lieut. PINSER went forward but was unable to get as man as forward as GUILLEMONT	
		4.40 PM	Opened fire in support of Infantry attack on GUILLEMONT but not being able to find an enemy who were hidden in the sunken road their batteries were firing on the same target & the enemy suffered severely	

WAR DIARY
or
INTELLIGENCE SUMMARY

Army Form C. 2118

C.R.S.! Arty
30th Division

Place	Date	Hour	Summary of Events and Information	Remarks and references to Appendices
2/151	31/7/16		very heavily. Fired our barrage lines at irregular intervals during the night	

Myron Bre Ma.
Comdg 151/A.B.

30th Divisional Artillery

151st BRIGADE

ROYAL FIELD ARTILLERY.

AUGUST 1 9 1 6

Includes "A"; "B" & "C" Batteries.

WAR DIARY
or
INTELLIGENCE SUMMARY

(Erase heading not required.)

Army Form C. 2118

A/15/
30th Division

Place	Date	Hour	Summary of Events and Information	Remarks and references to Appendices
18/8/16				
	19/8/16		Battery marched to new Waggon Lines. NE of BETHUNE. Two guns went out into action on the march about 1 mile due East of GORRE village. Two more guns went out into position as registered on following day. Rest of the time spent in improving gun position	
	23/8/16	noon	Took over our position of the line from A/14/8. Zone extended from A9c5.0 to A8d6.2 chief characteristic being the large extent on the Southern half	
	23 to 30/8		No event of special importance occurred. Normal conditions of trench warfare. Received our S.O.S. call. Fired about 1150 rounds. There were no casualties during the month.	
			Between 19th & 31st 2 Lieut BRINDLE-KELLY posted to X/30 Trench Mortar Battery 2 Lieut E J PAYNE posted to this Bty with effect from 21/7/16	
29/8/16			Rec'd notification of re-organization of div Arty, 4 gun 18 pdr batteries to be converted into 6 gun batteries, to do this the 151st Bde ceases to exist	

WAR DIARY
or
INTELLIGENCE SUMMARY

Army Form C. 2118

B/151 Bhy
30th Division

Place	Date	Hour	Summary of Events and Information	Remarks and references to Appendices
B/151	13/9/16		2/Lieut Jas Douglas Bell joined the Battery	
	30/8/16		Brig General G.H.A. WHITE inspected horses	
			No.28905 Bomb. E.E. EGGLETON name appeared in the List of N.C.O's & men awarded the MILITARY MEDAL for acts of bravery	
B/151	1/9/16		Came out of action & joined the remainder of this Bde. concentrated in the BOIS de TAILLES	
	6/9/16	7 AM	Marched to LONGEAU and entrained detrained at MERVILLE same day, & proceeded to new billets near St VENANT	
	8/9/16		General T.S. SHEA C.B. D.S.O. addressed the Bde. complimenting them on the work done at the SOMME	
	10/9/16		Inspection of horses by the P.V.O who said they were very good & the best Battery of horses on the division	
	11/9/16		Rested at St VENANT until the 11th when the Bty marched to new billets at M-- BERNENSHON, where I rested until the 18th	

WAR DIARY
or
INTELLIGENCE SUMMARY
(Erase heading not required.)

Army Form C. 2118

B/151
30. L. Division

Place	Date	Hour	Summary of Events and Information	Remarks and references to Appendices
BOIS du TAILLES	1/7/16	10 PM	Battery came out of action, & proceeded to Major Line of BRONFAY FARM	
	3/7/16	6 PM	Moved off at 6 P.M. to join the rest of the 151 Bde at the BOIS des TAILLES, marched via CORBIE & LA NEUVILLE to DAOURS, encamping in wood near the town	
	5/7/16	10 AM	Stayed at DAOURS till night 4. 5/6. Marched to LONGEAU to entrain, which was done very expeditiously. Travelled by train to MERVILLE where the battery detrained. Marched to a place about 2 miles due east of Qt VENANT in the FIRST ARMY area.	
	5/7/16		General J.S. SHEA. CB DSO addressed the Brigade, complimenting them on work during the recent operations. Horses inspected by the P.V.O.	
	10/8/16			
	12/9/16		Battery marched to LES HARISOIRS about 3 miles north of BETHUNE & just south of the LA BASSEE CANAL	
	26/9/16		Orders received for reorganization of Artillery, all 18 pdr batteries to be increased to 6 guns. This was done by taking over a section of C Battery	

Army Form C. 2118

WAR DIARY
or
INTELLIGENCE SUMMARY
(Erase heading not required.)

C/151 Bty.
30th Division

Place	Date	Hour	Summary of Events and Information	Remarks and references to Appendices
Br Stables Trench MARICOURT	1/8/16		Firing on various targets throughout the day (harassed by the Valley SE of GUILLEMONT (T 26 d) firing salvos at irregular intervals. The valley in A 10 the BRIQUETERIE Rd & the Battery position were heavily shelled during the night 31/7/16 to 1/8/16. Major N.A.L. DAY & 9 gunners were wounded & 7 horses killed. Ammunition Wagon totally destroyed. Action in the early morning.	
		10.15 PM	Relief of C/375 relieved Nos 2 & 3 guns which were left out of The night picket of Battery completed & guns returned to Wagon Lines.	
	2/8/16		Wagon line moved to BOIS des TAILLES (North) 2nd Lieut A.O. GILBY joined	
	3/8/16	7.30 AM	BATTERY moved out of B. de T. at 7.30 AM & marched to DAOURS arriving about noon. Bivouaced on side of road South of the village	
DAOURS	4/8/16	12 noon	Resting at DAOURS	
	5/8/16		Battery moved out of DAOURS at 12 midnight & marched to LONGEAU	

WAR DIARY or INTELLIGENCE SUMMARY

Army Form C. 2118

B/151
30 Divisions

Place	Date	Hour	Summary of Events and Information	Remarks and references to Appendices
LONGEAU	6/5/16	6.30 AM	Entrained at LONGEAU. Buffers arranged much for entraining Battery	
		8.30	Train left LONGEAU, arrived at THIENNES at 5 AM & unloaded Horses to billets 2½ miles due east of Qt VENANT. Resting at Qt VENANT. Inspection of horses on 10/5 by P.V.O. 14 animals sent to 40th Mobile Vet Sect	
	7-10			
	11/5/16		Marched out of Qt VENANT at 2.30 PM to new wagon lines about 1 mile east of HINGES. From this date Battery was refitting & training. All four guns were sent to the 1 O.M. workshops at BETHUNE & taken down & overhauled	
	14/5/16		Major F.L.C. LIVINGSTONE-LEARMONTH took over command of the Battery	
	20/5/16		Orders given for re-organization of R.F.A. to 6 gun Batteries under which the 151st Bde ceases to exist. The right section of this Battery joining A/151 to be constituted into new C/149. Left section to join B/151 to constitute new B/149. 2/Lieut R.F. Penn posted to R.F.C. with effect from 11/5/16 having been attached on probation since 5/5/16	

1875 Wt. W393/826 1,000,000 4/15 J.B.C. & A. A.D.S.S./Forms/C. 2118.

(WAR DIARY or INTELLIGENCE SUMMARY — Army Form C. 2118)

151 Bde
30th Division

Place	Date	Hour	Summary of Events and Information	Remarks and references to Appendices
BERMANSHON	31/8/16		A. Bty. together with 1 section of C Bty. became B/148	
			B. " " " " " " " " B/149	
			Major F.L.C LIVINGSTONE-LEARMONTH to command C/148	
			Capt H.B. IMBERT-TERRY to command B/149	
	31/8/16		The Bde Hd Qrs divided up as follows —	
			1 NCO & 2 men to Sub Bty Hd Qrs	
			1 " 2 " to D/148	
			2 " 4 " to H.Q.149	
			2 " 1 " to H.Q.150	
			3 " 4 " to C/148	
			2 " 11 " to C/149	
			1 " 4 " to B/149	
			1 W.O. — to D.A.C	
			All Vehicles to D.A.C	
			Return to D.A.D.O.S	
			Horses divided between D.A.C B/149 & C/148	

C.J.O. Lt. Col. CE 151/A/5

30ᵃ

150 RFA
vol 4

157st Bde: R.FA.
Vol. 3

3d

WO 95
23211 7
JUN 1917 - OCT 1918
TRENCH MORTAR SUPPLIES

www.ingramcontent.com/pod-product-compliance
Lightning Source LLC
Chambersburg PA
CBHW081437160426
43193CB00013B/2311